BHAGAVAD GITA
ILLUSTRATED AND ADAPTED FOR YOUNG READERS

DINESH DECKKER

SUBHASHINI SUMANASEKARA

First Published in 2023 IN USA

© Dinsu Books

Book Designed by: Dinesh Deckker

ISBN-13 : 9798340158482

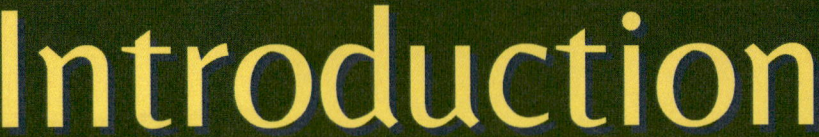

Introduction

The Bhagavad Gita is a special talk between a warrior named Arjuna and a wise teacher named Krishna. They talk on a big battlefield, but they're not just talking about fighting. They talk about life, making choices, and doing the right thing.

In this book, we make this big story simple so kids like you can understand it. You'll learn how to be brave, make smart choices, and see how your actions matter. Each chapter has a new lesson and colorful pictures to show you what's happening. Let's start this adventure and learn from Krishna's wisdom!

THIS BOOK IS DEDICATED TO OUR PRINCESS SASHA.

Kurukshetra was a big, dusty field where two groups, the Pandavas and the Kauravas, were ready to fight. The field was full of warriors, horses, elephants, and chariots. Colorful flags flew in the sky, and the ground had marks from the chariots. Everyone was nervous and waiting for the big battle.

But something very special happened here. Lord Krishna spoke to Arjuna and taught him about being brave and doing the right thing. Even though it was a battlefield, Kurukshetra became a place where we learned important lessons about life.

Arjuna's Confusion

As Arjuna stands on the battlefield, he sees his family, friends, and teachers on the other side. He is filled with sadness and fear. How can he fight against people he loves? He turns to Krishna for help.

The Eternal Soul

Krishna explains to Arjuna that the soul is eternal and does not die. The body may perish, but the soul lives on. Krishna encourages Arjuna to do his duty and fight for what is right.

The Path of Selfless Action

Krishna teaches Arjuna about "Karma Yoga," the path of selfless action. He explains that we should do our duties without expecting rewards or worrying about the results. When we act selflessly, we help the world.

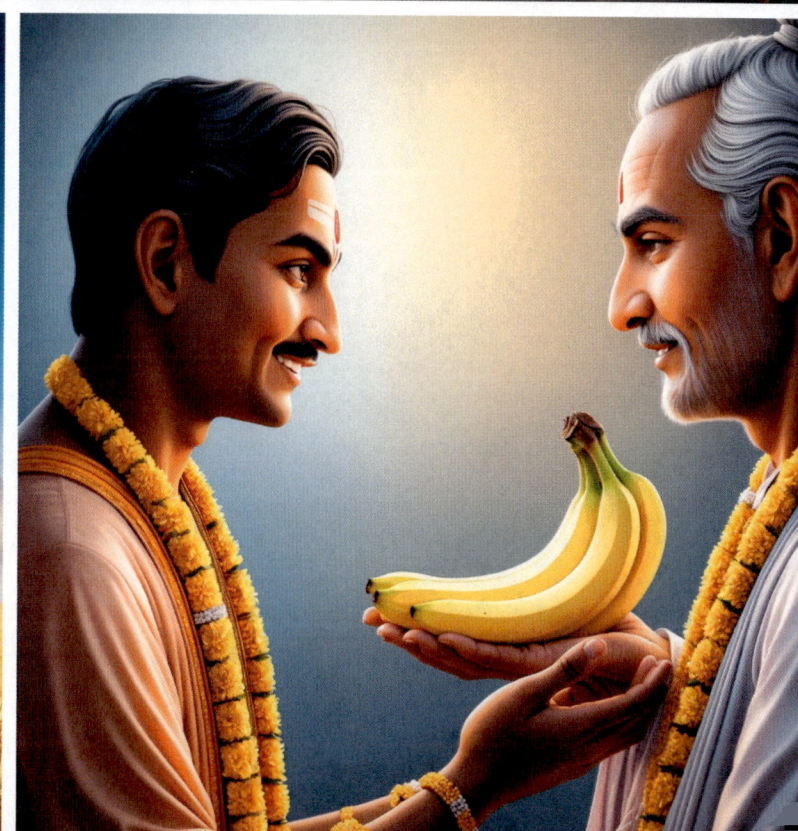

The Wisdom of Time

Krishna reveals that he has taught this knowledge to others in the past. He tells Arjuna that he has lived many lives, just like everyone else, and each life is a chance to learn and grow.

Krishna is timeless.

True Freedom

Krishna explains that true freedom comes from letting go of attachment to success and failure. A wise person stays calm no matter what happens, and this calmness brings peace.

The Power of Meditation

Krishna tells Arjuna that meditation is a way to control the mind and make it peaceful. A person who meditates learns how to focus on what is important and keep their mind calm, even in difficult times.

Knowing God

Krishna explains that everything in the world comes from him—the sky, the earth, the people, and animals. He is present in everything, and by understanding this, we can feel closer to God.

The Eternal Journey of the Soul

Krishna explains the journey of the soul after death. The choices we make in life affect what happens to our soul, and living a life of kindness and duty leads to peace.

The Secret of Devotion

Krishna tells Arjuna that anyone who loves and serves God will always be protected. It doesn't matter how powerful or rich someone is; what matters is their love and devotion.

Krishna's Divine Glory

Krishna reveals his divine nature to Arjuna, showing that he is not just a charioteer, but the Supreme Being who is part of everything in the universe. He controls everything and is the source of all strength and wisdom.

The Universal Form

Krishna shows Arjuna his "Vishvarupa" or Universal Form, a mighty and powerful vision where Krishna appears in his true, magnificent form. Arjuna realizes the vastness of Krishna's power.

The Path of Love and Devotion

Krishna tells Arjuna that the easiest way to reach him is through love and devotion. When we love God and are kind to others, we become closer to God and to peace.

The Field and the Knower

Krishna explains that the body is like a field, and the soul is the knower of this field.

By understanding the difference between the body and the soul, we can live wisely.

The Three Qualities of Life

Krishna explains that everything in life has three qualities: goodness, passion, and ignorance. By understanding these qualities, we can live a balanced life and choose goodness over the other qualities.

GOODNESS

PASSION

IGNORANCE

The Tree of Life

Krishna describes life as a great tree with deep roots. He explains that to find peace, we must cut the attachments that tie us to this tree and seek the divine instead.

The Nature of Good and Evil

Krishna tells Arjuna that there are two kinds of people in the world: those who follow the path of good, and those who follow the path of evil.
It is important to choose goodness to live a happy and peaceful life.

Faith and Belief

Krishna explains that different people have different kinds of faith, based on what they believe. Some have strong faith, while others are unsure. But the most important thing is to have faith in doing good.

The Final Teaching

In the final chapter, Krishna reminds Arjuna that the greatest thing he can do is to trust in God and do his duty without fear. Krishna promises to always protect those who trust in him.

Conclusion

The Bhagavad Gita teaches us that life is a journey of learning, growing, and making the right choices. Through Arjuna's story, we learn how to face challenges with wisdom, courage, and love. By doing good and staying calm in difficult times, we can find peace and happiness, just like Arjuna did with Krishna's guidance.

A Message from Authors to Children

As we close the pages of our journey through the Bhagavad Gita, we hope you found inspiration in the stories of Arjuna and his divine guide, Krishna. Their conversations teach us not just about the battles we face outside, but also about conquering the challenges within ourselves.

Remember, like Arjuna, you too can find courage and wisdom with the help of good friends and thoughtful guidance. Keep these stories in your heart as you meet your own challenges, knowing that you have the strength to choose wisely and act kindly.

Thank you for joining us on this epic adventure. May the lessons of the Gita light your path to greatness and peace.
Until our next adventure,

With warm wishes and love, Dinesh & Subhashini

DINESH DECKKER

AUTHOR

Dinesh Deckker is a multifaceted author and educator with a rich academic background and extensive experience in creative writing and education. Holding a BSc Hons in Computer Science, a BA (Hons), and an MBA from prestigious institutions in the UK, Dinesh has dedicated his career to blending technology, education, and literature.

BA, MBA (UK), PhD (Student)

He has further honed his writing skills through a variety of specialized courses. His qualifications include:

- Children Acquiring Literacy Naturally from UC Santa Cruz, USA
- Creative Writing Specialization from Wesleyan University, USA
- Writing for Young Readers Commonwealth Education Trust
- Introduction to Early Childhood from The State University of New York
- Introduction to Psychology from Yale University
- Academic English: Writing Specialization University of California, Irvine,
- Writing and Editing Specialization from University of Michigan
- Writing and Editing: Word Choice University of Michigan
- Sharpened Visions: A Poetry Workshop from CalArts, USA
- Grammar and Punctuation from University of California, Irvine, USA
- Teaching Writing Specialization from Johns Hopkins University
- Advanced Writing from University of California, Irvine, USA
- English for Journalism from University of Pennsylvania, USA
- Creative Writing: The Craft of Character from Wesleyan University, USA
- Creative Writing: The Craft of Setting from Wesleyan University
- Creative Writing: The Craft of Plot from Wesleyan University, USA
- Creative Writing: The Craft of Style from Wesleyan University, USA

Dinesh's diverse educational background and commitment to lifelong learning have equipped him with a deep understanding of various writing styles and educational techniques. His works often reflect his passion for storytelling, education, and technology, making him a versatile and engaging author.

SUBHASHINI SUMANASEKARA
AUTHOR

With more than 20 years of expertise, Subhashini Sumanasekara is a renowned ICT educator committed to mentoring students from a variety of backgrounds. Her experience in the industry is further enhanced by her Master of Science in Strategic IT Management from the University of Wolverhampton.

BSc, MSc (UK), PhD (Student)

Made in the USA
Coppell, TX
05 June 2025

50387650R00031